Watching and Waiting
What Hatches from Nature's Nurseries

Sara Levine

Millbrook Press / Minneapolis

For Mona

Text copyright © 2025 by Sara Levine

All rights reserved. International copyright secured. No part of this book may be reproduced, stored in a retrieval system, or transmitted in any form or by any means—electronic, mechanical, photocopying, recording, or otherwise—without the prior written permission of Lerner Publishing Group, Inc., except for the inclusion of brief quotations in an acknowledged review.

Millbrook Press™
An imprint of Lerner Publishing Group, Inc.
241 First Avenue North
Minneapolis, MN 55401 USA

For reading levels and more information, look up this title at www.lernerbooks.com.

Image credits: Nature Picture Library/Alamy, pp. 1, 28 (ostrich egg), 31; FatCamera/Getty Images, p. 3; Suphat phalasoon/Shutterstock, pp. 5, 28 (snake eggs); piemags/nature/Alamy, pp. 6, 29 (witch hazel gall), 15, 29 (wool sower gall); AleMasche72/Getty Images, pp. 9, 29 (oak gall); Werner Meidinger/Alamy, p. 11, 29 (silk button gall); Marc Andreu/Shutterstock, p. 12, 28 (slug eggs); Михаил Жигалин/Alamy, pp. 16, 28 (mantis egg case); LumineImages/Shutterstock, p. 19; diane555/Getty Images, pp. 20, 28 (goldenrod gall); Giliane Mansfeldt/Independent Picture Service, pp. 21, 30 (bottom); Alistair Berg/Getty Images, p. 22; Africanway/Getty Images, pp. 23, 28; Avalon.red/Alamy, pp. 25, 28 (butterfly egg); KMWiggins/Getty Images, p. 26; photoguns/Getty Images, p. 27; Julian Nieman/Alamy, p. 28 (slug); Teresa Kopec/Getty Images, p. 28 (ostrich); John Sullivan/Alamy, p. 28 (snake); Dany Store/Shutterstock, p. 28 (bullfrog); Jan Jirsa/Shutterstock, p. 28 (butterfly); Paul Starosta/Getty Images, p. 28 (praying mantis); Tom Applegate/Getty Images, p. 28 (quail); victoriabee/Getty Images, p. 28 (quail eggs); Vinícius Souza/Alamy, p. 29 (midge); Beatriz Moisset (CC BY-ND-NC 1.0), p. 29 (aphid); Natthager/Wikimedia Commons (CC BY-SA 4.0), p. 29 (wasp 1); Protasov AN/Shutterstock, p. 29 (wasp 2); Nick Furlan (CC BY-NC 4.0), p. 29 (wasp 3); Matthijs Wetterauw/Alamy, p. 29 (beech gall); skitterbug (CC BY 4.0), p. 29 (fly); United Archives GmbH/Alamy, p. 30 (top). Design Element: Anna Timoshenko/Shutterstock.

Cover: Matthijs Wetterauw/Alamy; victoriabee/Getty Images.

Designed by Emily Harris.
Main body text set in Tw Cen MT Std. Typeface provided by Monotype Typography.

Library of Congress Cataloging-in-Publication Data

Names: Levine, Sara (Veterinarian), author.
Title: Watching and waiting: what hatches from nature's nurseries / Sara Levine.
Description: Minneapolis: Millbrook Press, [2025] | Includes bibliographical references. | Audience: Ages 4–9 | Audience: Grades 2–3 |
  Summary: "What should you do if you find eggs, egg cases, or galls when you're exploring the outdoors? You could wait and watch and even come back to check on them to see what emerges" —Provided by publisher.
Identifiers: LCCN 2024023807 (print) | LCCN 2024023808 (ebook) | ISBN 9798765648940 (lib. bdg.) | ISBN 9798765659274 (epub)
Subjects: LCSH: Eggs—Juvenile literature. | Embryology—Juvenile literature. | Animals—Infancy—Juvenile literature.
Classification: LCC QL956.5 .L48 2025 (print) | LCC QL956.5 (ebook) | DDC 591.4/68—dc23/eng/20240722

LC record available at https://lccn.loc.gov/2024023807
LC ebook record available at https://lccn.loc.gov/2024023808

Manufactured in the United States of America
1-1011026-53493-10/31/2024

When you find something
interesting and beautiful . . .

Resting in a shallow nest of soil,

Or rising up like tiny witches' hats from the surface of a leaf,

Round and smooth
like a marble,

Or like cereal glued to the underside of a leaf,

slug eggs

Tiny and translucent
and damp and perfect,

Or fluffy and white
and dotted with pink,

praying mantis egg case

You might be tempted to open it to find out what's growing inside.

But if you do, what's **inside** will not grow anymore. It will die.

Instead, you could **wait**.
Leave what you've found where it is.

goldenrod gall

goldenrod gall

Or place it in a jar with gauze on top and keep it **safe**.

You can come back and **check** every day.

Until the mystery **reveals** itself.

frog eggs

Things that were meant to be will **hatch** out, given the right conditions and the right amount of **time**.

large white butterfly eggs and larvae

Sometimes the best thing a scientist can do is **protect** and **observe**

robin eggs

and **wait** to see what emerges.

What Is an Egg?

An egg is a container in which an animal grows. The animal hatches out when it's ready to be in the world. Eggs come in all different shapes and sizes. Animals that lay eggs include birds, turtles, beetles, and fish. Can you think of some other animals that lay eggs?

The eggs in this book include these:

Ostrich egg

Snake eggs

Slug eggs

Frog eggs

Butterfly egg

Quail eggs

What Is an Egg Case?

An egg case is a container that holds many eggs. Egg cases come in interesting shapes and sizes. A praying mantis mother makes a foamy liquid when she is laying her eggs. It hardens into a case to protect the eggs until they hatch.

Other animals that make interesting egg cases include spiders, whelks, and skates.

A praying mantis egg case is shown in this book.

Praying mantis egg case

What Is a Gall?

A gall is a bump that forms in a plant, creating a special place for an insect to grow. How does this happen? Usually, a mother insect or mite inserts some chemicals into the plant along with her eggs. The chemicals cause the plant to grow a safe home around her eggs. When the babies hatch out, they have shelter and food to eat. They chew their way out of the gall when they are ready to leave.

Insects that commonly form galls include wasps, midges, and aphids.

Each gall looks different depending on which animal made it. So if you find one and have a good field guide, you can guess which animal will emerge.

There are other ways galls can grow in a plant. Fungus, bacteria, or other diseases can make plants form galls too.

The galls in this book include these:

What Is Observational Science?

There are a lot of ways to learn about living things. Some scientists choose to observe in a way that will not hurt animals or interfere with their lives. They just watch and wait to learn. One scientist who is famous for learning about animals in this way is Jane Goodall (*shown at right*). She discovered many things about chimpanzees by watching them in the wild.

Activities

Be an Observational Scientist

You don't need to wait until you grow up to be a scientist. You can start observing now.

Go outside and look for eggs, egg cases, and galls. Look under logs. Maybe you'll find some slug eggs.

Look closely at plants and trees. Do you notice any unusual bumps? If you do, it might be a gall.

Look closely at tall grasses at the edges of fields. Maybe you will find a praying mantis egg case.

Watch wild animals outside. Find an animal that is very common where you live. Maybe an ant or a bird? Pick one to watch, and see what it does. Where does it go? Is it interacting with any other animals? Do you see signs of what it is eating? Or where it is laying eggs? Bring a notebook and pencil so you can write down everything you notice and make some sketches of the animal.

Observing Eggs, Egg Cases, and Galls Indoors

Most eggs, egg cases, and galls do better outside where their mothers choose to lay them. But if you follow these steps, you can try bringing some of them inside safely to observe them and see if the young hatch out. Here's what you need:

- A clean container such as a jar or an aquarium tank
- Layers of paper towels
- A spray bottle with water
- Gauze, such as cheesecloth, to cover the container
- Hair elastic or string to hold gauze on
- Paper and pencil or a camera for recording observations

Caring for Slug Eggs Indoors

Most eggs need to be under precise temperatures to hatch, so usually it's safer to let eggs grow and hatch outside. But slug eggs are one exception because they are easy to care for in a container.

1. Look under rocks, bricks, or logs to find slug eggs.
2. Carefully scoop them up along with the dirt around them, and place them into your container.
3. Cover the dirt with wet paper towels.
4. Check each day to make sure the soil and paper towels are damp. If they aren't, spray more water on them.
5. When the baby slugs emerge, take a close look at them. Write down observations, and draw pictures or take photos.
6. Finally, let them go. Put them back where you found them on the day they hatch out so they can find everything they need to survive.

Caring for a Gall or Egg Case Inside

1. Find an egg case or a gall in nature.
2. Break off the part of the plant it is growing on, leaving a large part of the stem or leaf it is on intact, and place it gently into your container.
3. Add damp paper towels to the bottom of your container, with the egg case or gall resting on top.
4. Check each day that the paper towels are still damp. If not, spray them with more water.
5. When the insects emerge, take a close look at them.* Write down observations, and draw pictures or take photos.
6. Finally, let them go. Put them back where you found them on the day they hatch out so they can find everything they need to survive.**

*Some of the insect babies will look like larvae, not like their adult selves.
**If you keep praying mantis babies too long, they will get hungry and eat one another!

Babies emerging from praying mantis egg case

Further Learning

Books for Young Readers

Arnold, Caroline. *Hatching Chicks in Room 6*. Watertown, MA: Charlesbridge, 2017.

Aston, Dianna Hutts. *An Egg Is Quiet*. Illustrated by Sylvia Long. San Francisco: Chronicle Books, 2014.

Jenkins, Steve, and Robin Page. *Egg: Nature's Perfect Package*. Illustrated by Steve Jenkins. Boston: Houghton Mifflin Harcourt, 2015.

Meisel, Paul. *My Awesome Summer by P. Mantis*. New York: Holiday House, 2018.

Posada, Mia. *Guess What Is Growing Inside This Egg*. Minneapolis: Millbrook Press, 2007.

Winter, Jeanette. *The Watcher: Jane Goodall's Life with Chimps*. New York: Schwartz & Wade Books, 2011.

Resources for Learning with Adults

Eiseman, Charley, and Noah Charney. *Tracks & Sign of Insects and Other Invertebrates: A Guide to North American Species*. Mechanicsburg, PA: Stackpole Books, 2010.

"How to Hatch/Care for Praying Mantis Eggs!" YouTube video, 5:13. Posted by Pablo Hunt, April 7, 2021. https://www.youtube.com/watch?v=Drf5so7XJQA.

Redfern, Margaret, and R. R. Askew. *Plant Galls*. Slough, UK: Richmond, 1992.

Russo, Ronald A. *Plant Galls of the Western United States*. Princeton, NJ: Princeton University Press, 2021.

Stokes, Donald W. *Stokes Guide to Observing Insect Lives*. Illustrated by Deborah Prince. New York: Little, Brown, 1983.